| Zac Newton Investigates |

Extraordinary Electricity

WORLD BOOK

www.worldbook.com

World Book, Inc.
180 North LaSalle Street
Suite 900
Chicago, Illinois 60601
USA

For information about other World Book publications, visit our website at www.worldbook.com or call 1-800-WORLDBK (967-5325).

For information about sales to schools and libraries, call 1-800-975-3250 (United States), or 1-800-837-5365 (Canada).

© 2018 (print and e-book) by World Book, Inc. All rights reserved. No part of this publication may be reproduced, stored in a retrieval system, or transmitted in any form or by any means (electronic, mechanical, photocopying, recording, or otherwise) without written permission from World Book, Inc.

WORLD BOOK and the GLOBE DEVICE are registered trademarks or trademarks of World Book, Inc.

Library of Congress Cataloging-in-Publication Data for this volume has been applied for.

This edition: ISBN: 978-0-7166-4058-5 (hc.)
ISBN: 978-0-7166-4056-1 (set, hc.)

Also available as: ISBN: 978-0-7166-4064-6 (e-book)

Printed in China by Shenzhen Wing King Tong Paper Products Co., Ltd., Shenzhen, Guangdong
1st printing July 2018

Produced for World Book by White-Thomson Publishing Ltd
www.wtpub.co.uk

Author: Paul Harrison
Editor: Izzi Howell
Design/Art director: Claire Gaukrodger
Illustrator: Rob Davis/The Art Agency

Cover artwork: © Doug Holgate

Staff

Executive Committee

President
Jim O'Rourke

Vice President and Editor in Chief
Paul A. Kobasa

Vice President, Finance
Donald D. Keller

Vice President, Marketing
Jean Lin

Vice President, International Sales
Maksim Rutenberg

Vice President, Technology
Jason Dole

Director, Human Resources
Bev Ecker

Editorial

Director, New Print
Tom Evans

Managing Editor
Jeff De La Rosa

Librarian
S. Thomas Richardson

Manager, Contracts & Compliance (Rights & Permissions)
Loranne K. Shields

Manager, Indexing Services
David Pofelski

Digital

Director, Digital Product Development
Erika Meller

Manager, Digital Products
Jonathan Wills

Graphics and Design

Senior Art Director
Tom Evans

Senior Web Designer/Digital Media Developer
Matt Carrington

Manufacturing/Production

Manufacturing Manager
Anne Fritzinger

Proofreader
Nathalie Strassheim

A glossary of terms appears on p. 94.

Contents

- **6** Chapter 1: Orbit Bolts
- **14** Chapter 2: Franklin Flies a Kite
- **22** Chapter 3: All That Static
- **32** Chapter 4: Blackout
- **37** Chapter 5: Animal Electricity
- **45** Chapter 6: Battery Power
- **54** Chapter 7: A Magnetic Idea
- **63** Chapter 8: Cracking the Code
- **73** Chapter 9: Current Events
- **86** Chapter 10: Power Up
- **92** Meet the Scientists
- **94** Glossary
- **95** Additional Resources
- **96** Index

Zac Newton and friends

Zac is a junior genius and inventor of the Backspace app. The app allows Zac and his friends to take virtual trips through time and space, just by snapping a selfie.

Lucía has a sharp mind and an even sharper wit. She pretends to be too cool for school, but inside she burns to learn about science.

Quick-thinking Marcus is always ready with a joke. Although he loves to clown around, he knows more than he lets on.

Ning likes to run, jump, and play ball. She may be the youngest of the group, but nobody's going to push her around.

Zac's dog, Orbit, loves to join Zac and his friends on their adventures. He's not afraid of anything—except loud noises.

Chapter 1
Orbit Bolts

"Hey, look! Isn't that Orbit?" Lucía shouted. She was looking out the window of Marcus's house when she saw the dog run past. "Where's he going?"

Lightning flashed, and thunder rumbled in the distance.

"I remember Zac saying that Orbit is afraid of thunder," Marcus replied. "Come on, let's see if we can catch him." Marcus paused at the screen door, worried. "I hope we can get him before it starts raining."

"They're just raindrops, Marcus," Lucía teased. "I promise you won't melt."

Lucía dashed out the door, and Marcus followed. The two children sprinted down the street. They chased the dog past several blocks of houses and into a park.

"Orbit!" Lucía shouted. Heavy raindrops began to splash down all around them. "Come here, boy!"

Marcus whistled to get Orbit's attention. Orbit just ran in circles, barking at the thunder.

"Ugh, I'm getting soaked! Let's get under here!" Marcus said. He and Lucía ducked under a tall, leafy tree.

"Over here, Orbit!" Marcus shouted. Finally, Orbit ran to him and Lucía.

"Orbit, I know you don't like storms, but you can't run away like that! Where's Zac?" Marcus ruffled the dog's damp fur. He looked around the park for any sign of Zac Newton.

Lightning flashed in the sky. Orbit tried to run, but Marcus had a good grip on his collar. "We should get out of here before the storm gets worse," Marcus said. "It looks like it's gonna be a big one."

"Hey! Get out from under there!" they heard Zac Newton yell. He came running across the park.

"Thanks for catching Orbit," Zac panted. "I've been chasing him since the thunder started. He cut through a yard and lost me. Come on, let's get to my house before we get zapped by lightning!"

Marcus and Lucía followed Zac and Orbit. They made it to Zac's house just as it really began to pour. Angry lightning crackled overhead.

"Come into the kitchen and dry off," said Zac. He grabbed some towels from a drawer and tossed them to Marcus and Lucía.

Ning was sitting at Zac's kitchen table, looking at an old piece of paper covered in strange markings. "Before Orbit took off, Ning and I were trying to figure out what's on this paper she found in her attic," said Zac.

"Hi, there!" called Ning. "What were you doing out in the rain?"

"Hey, Ning. Just playing with the dog," Marcus joked. He patted his face with the towel.

Zac tried to towel off Orbit. The dog backed off and shook vigorously, showering the children with water.

"I'm glad we got away from those trees," Zac said. "Lightning will shock your shoes off. Under a tree is one of the worst places to be when there's lightning. You know what a bolt of electricity like that can do, right?"

"Well, I know lightning is dangerous," replied Marcus, "but I don't like getting rained on. Taking cover under the tree seemed like a good idea."

"You bet lightning is dangerous," Zac said. "Lightning is a giant electric spark."

"Is that the same as the electricity we use in lights and televisions and things?" Ning asked.

"Yes, like that, but lightning is much stronger," Zac replied. "During a storm, all these little particles of ice and water are blowing around inside the clouds. All that energy causes electric charges to build up in different areas of the cloud. When the charges become strong enough, electric energy can jump from one place to another—in the form of a lightning bolt. Sometimes, lightning shoots from cloud to cloud. Other times, it strikes tall things on the ground, like buildings."

"Or trees," Marcus said.

"Right. That's why you shouldn't hide under a tree during a storm," Zac said.

"How strong is lightning?" Lucía asked.

"Well," said Zac, "lightning is amazing stuff. It can

carry a charge of about 100 million volts. An ordinary flashlight, by comparison, uses about one and a half volts. All that energy heats the air around a lightning bolt to around 55,000 degrees Fahrenheit—that's 30,000 degrees Celsius."

Marcus laughed, "Last week, my dad baked a cake at 350 degrees Fahrenheit. So, I guess we would be pretty scorched if we got hit by 55,000-degree lightning."

"Okay, Zac, if you're so smart, where does the thunder come from?" Lucía asked.

"All that heat causes the air around the lightning to expand, or spread out, really fast," Zac explained. "The expanding air crashes into the air around it, making vibrations. To us, the vibrations sound like rumbles or cracks."

A flash of lightning crackled outside the window. Thunder boomed across the sky overhead.

Zac's face lit up. "Hey, this reminds me of a story about Benjamin Franklin. Let's use my Backspace app to pay him a visit."

The Backspace app was Zac's greatest invention. It could take Zac and his friends on a virtual visit to any point in history.

"Ben Franklin? You mean that old guy whose picture is on the hundred-dollar bill?" asked Lucía.

"We learned about him in history class," Marcus added. "He signed the Declaration of Independence and the Constitution. But what does that have to do with electricity?"

"Besides all that, Ben Franklin was a great inventor," explained Zac. "He created the Franklin stove and a kind of eyeglasses called bifocals, too. He started inventing things when he was young."

"Just like you, Zac!" Ning said.

"I'll thank him for the glasses while we're in the neighborhood," Marcus joked, adjusting the square frames of his own glasses.

Zac pulled his cell phone from his pocket and opened the Backspace app. "Okay, you all remember how this works?" he asked. "Gather around, and I'll take a selfie. Remember to gather close. If you don't make it into the picture, you'll get left behind. I'll type in our destination."

"This is going to be awesome!" Ning said. "It's been a while since we went on an adventure."

"Alright, it's ready," Zac said. The children huddled together. Zac's held the phone in his outstretched hand. They looked into it.

"Here we go!" Zac tapped the Backspace button, and the camera's flash lit up the room.

FLASH!

ZUMMMMMMmmmmmmm...

Chapter 2
Franklin Flies a Kite

When the flash faded, the children were standing in an open wooden building in the middle of a field. Rain poured down around them.

"What is this place?" asked Ning.

"It's a cow shelter," said Zac. He pointed to a couple of cows resting in the hay nearby.

Near the shelter door, two men huddled together. They held onto their hats as strong winds blew across the field.

"That's Ben Franklin and his son William," Zac said. "Franklin thinks that lightning is made up of electricity, but he hasn't found a way to prove it. So he's flying a kite in a storm, hoping to capture some electricity from the lightning."

"Isn't that incredibly dangerous?" Lucía asked

"It is," Zac replied. "One scientist had already died trying to do the same experiment. Ben Franklin got lucky. His kite merely picked up a low level of electric charge from the stormy air. The scientist who died was probably zapped by a direct lightning strike, which is much stronger."

Zac continued, "Also, check out what Ben's kite is made of."

The children moved to the edge of the shelter and looked up. A diamond-shaped kite whipped back and forth high above. Its frame was covered in silk. A metal wire was attached to the top of the frame, pointing straight up. The long kite string stretched down to Ben Franklin's hands. Pulling hard against the wind, Franklin handed the string to his son. While his son held the kite, Ben tied a key to the string using a silk ribbon.

"When it comes to electricity, the conductor matters," Zac said.

"What's a conductor?" Ning asked.

"A conductor is a thing that carries electric current—a flow of electricity—from one place to another," Zac answered. "Most metals are good conductors, including copper, aluminum, silver, and even gold."

"Metal is a good conductor for electricity," Marcus repeated. "That's why he put the wire on top, and why he's using the metal key."

"That's right," Zac agreed. Lightning flashed and thunder shook the shelter. The children shivered in the wind and huddled closer together.

"Don't worry," Zac soothed. "We're not really here in this storm. This is just the Backspace app showing us what history was like. We can't be hurt by any of the things you see here. It's all virtual reality!"

Ben Franklin turned from his son, who struggled with the kite. "Oh, hello," Franklin called over the howling wind. "I didn't see you there!"

"Hello, Mr. Franklin!" Zac said. "How is the experiment going?"

"It's rather tricky!" Franklin replied. "It's hard to hold on to the kite in this strong wind."

"Will the experiment work with all this rain?" Marcus asked.

"Oh, yes!" Franklin replied. "Water conducts electricity very well! If lightning is electric in nature, as I believe it to be, the water will help the soaking wet kite string to conduct electric current from the wire up top to the key down here."

A wild gust of wind blew through the shelter. The kite bucked, and Franklin turned back to help his son. The kids watched anxiously as a flash of lightning crackled just beyond them.

The rough twine of the kite string was covered in tiny loose strands. As the children watched, the strands began to stand on end like short, frayed hairs.

"That's the electric charge building up in the string," Zac explained.

Ben Franklin reached out a hand toward the dangling key.

"Don't try this at home!" Zac shouted.

Suddenly, a spark jumped from the tip of the key to Mr. Franklin's hand. "It worked," Franklin shouted. "The electric charge on the kite string! The spark from the key! Solid evidence that lightning is electricity!" Father and son cheered excitedly as the wind whipped their hats off.

"Wow!" Ning shouted. "Did you see that? I can't believe we saw it happen!"

"That was amazing!" Lucía agreed.

"Come on!" Zac yelled over the thunder and roaring wind. "The storm is getting worse! Let's get back!" Zac tapped the screen of his phone, and the kids were suddenly back in his cozy kitchen.

Ning's eyes darted around the room, settling on a blender. "So, the same thing that makes up lightning is what we use to make this blender work?" she asked.

"That's right!" Zac replied.

"Then how come I don't get zapped when I touch its

cord, like Ben Franklin did when he touched the key?" Ning asked.

"The conductor is a metal wire inside the cord. It carries electric current from the power outlet to the blender's motor," Zac explained. "You don't get a shock from touching the cord because the wire is covered with rubber. Rubber is an insulator. An insulator is like the opposite of a conductor. Insulators resist the flow of electric current. Most materials that aren't metals are good insulators—especially rubber, wood, paper, glass, and even fibers like cotton."

"I get it," Ning said.

Marcus had grabbed Zac's phone, and he was looking up more information on Benjamin Franklin. "Sorry to change the subject," he interrupted, "but it says here that Ben Franklin invented the lightning rod as well."

"Right," Zac answered. "Ben Franklin invented the lightning rod after this experiment. They called it the Franklin rod. People added it to their houses to protect them against fires caused by lightning strikes."

"How did it do that?" Lucía asked.

"A lightning rod is a long metal pole you put on top of a building," Zac explained. "Remember that lightning tends to strike tall things? The metal rod attracts the lightning, which flows through a metal wire to the ground, rather than hitting the building."

"So, the lightning goes for the metal instead of the rooftop?" Marcus asked.

"Exactly! The lightning rod saved a lot of homes and buildings," Zac said. "Franklin's own house was saved by a lightning rod. That's what I call a lucky invention!"

Chapter 3
All That Static

Outside Zac's house, the storm continued. Clouds darkened the afternoon sky. Lightning flashed beyond the rain-streaked windows and lit up the kitchen.

"It's hard to believe that people didn't always have electricity," Ning said.

"Good thing Ben Franklin was smart enough to invent it for us," Marcus said.

Lucía gave him a look.

"Well, he didn't actually invent it," Marcus continued, "because it was always there. But he helped us to figure out what electricity is."

"I wonder when people first discovered electricity," Ning said.

"The ancient Greeks discovered electricity about 2,500 years ago," Zac said. "They rubbed pieces of a stone called amber with animal fur. This caused feathers and bits of straw to stick to the amber, from the static electricity."

"I've heard of static electricity," Lucía said. "It's that spark you get when you scuff your socks on the carpet and touch a doorknob, right?"

"That's part of it," Zac said. "But electricity is in everything. It is part of what makes up the world around us."

"Wait, what do you mean there's electricity in everything? I don't get a shock when I put on my shirt," Ning said jokingly, "or when I take a drink of milk."

"No," Zac replied, "but those things are made up of tiny pieces called atoms and molecules that are held together by… wait, let me show you." Zac grabbed a piece of paper and a pencil and sat down at the table. He began to sketch quickly as his friends watched.

"What are you drawing?" asked Ning.

"An atom," Zac replied.

"What's so interesting about atoms?" Ning said.

"Everything is made from atoms—millions and millions of them—your body, the shirt, milk... everything," Zac said.

"That's a lot of atoms," Ning replied.

"I'm drawing an atom," Zac continued, "a teeny, tiny piece of matter. Each atom has a nucleus, or core, like the pit of a peach." He drew a circle in the center of the paper. "It's the center that holds the rest of the atom together."

"Inside the nucleus, there are tiny bits called protons." Zac continued sketching. "Protons have a positive electric charge."

"What does that mean?" Marcus asked.

"There are two kinds of electric charge," Zac explained. "They are called *positive* and *negative*, and they are opposites. You've heard people say that opposites attract? Well, things with opposite electric charges attract each other. So something with a positive charge attracts, or pulls on, something with a negative charge."

"Okay, go on," said Marcus.

"So, we've got the nucleus, here, which is full of protons," Zac pointed to the drawing's center. Then he drew several smaller dots moving in circles around the nucleus. "These dots out here are electrons," Zac continued. "Electrons have a negative charge. They are attracted to the positively charged protons in the nucleus. Electrons have a tendency to zip through space. But, the attraction of the protons keeps them orbiting the nucleus, like Earth orbits the sun."

"WOOF!" Orbit barked.

"He thinks you're calling his name!" giggled Ning.

"Normally, an atom has an equal number of protons and electrons," Zac continued. "So the positive and negative charges equal out. The atom as a whole is not overly positive or negative. This is called being neutral."

"So, if it's neutral, that means there's no charge at all. Is that why we don't get a shock from putting on our shoes or taking a drink of milk?" Lucía asked.

"Exactly," Zac said. "But sometimes, like in a windy storm cloud, atoms bump into each other, and electrons get knocked from one atom to another. Some atoms end up with more electrons than protons, gaining a negative charge. Others have fewer electrons than protons, gaining a positive charge. Remember, opposites attract. The positively charged atoms pull on all those extra negatively charged electrons, causing them to jump back with a ZAP! In a cloud, that zap is the lightning."

The kids stared at the paper, scratching their heads.

Zac got up from the table and disappeared down the hallway. He returned with a big yellow balloon.

"What are you doing?" Ning asked.

Zac blew up the balloon and tied it off. "I'm going to show you static electricity in action." He rubbed the balloon gently on Orbit's back. Orbit gave them a curious look, his head tilted to one side.

"There are millions of atoms in Orbit's fur and in this balloon. Most of them were neutral, until I started rubbing the balloon on his fur. The rubbing shuffles the electrons around. Now, some of Orbit's electrons have rubbed off on the balloon, giving it a slight negative charge."

"And giving Orbit a slight positive charge," Ning giggled.

"Right," Zac said. "And with electricity, opposites attract. Positively charged atoms pull on all those extra electrons, and this happens… " Zac stopped rubbing and slowly pulled the balloon away from Orbit's back.

Orbit's fur stood on end, like it was trying to hold on to the balloon.

"See, the positively charged fur is attracted to the negatively charged balloon."

"Cool! Can I try?" Ning asked.

"Sure, just be gentle." Zac passed the balloon to Ning. She rubbed it on Orbit's back, squeezing it a bit too tight. POP! It snapped in her hand. Orbit ran for cover in the living room.

"Oops. Sorry," Ning said.

"No problem," said Zac. "Hey, I have an idea. Is everybody wearing socks?" The others looked at him, puzzled.

"Yeah, it looks like we're all covered in the sock

department," Marcus said, smiling. "What do you have in mind?"

"Let's just say my mom doesn't like shoes on the living room carpet. Take off your shoes and head into the living room. I'm going to see if I have another balloon," Zac said. He picked up his phone from the kitchen table and disappeared back into the hallway. He returned a moment later.

"Time to try out the Zoom In function on my app," Zac explained.

"How does that work?" Lucía asked.

"I'm going to zoom in on static electricity," Zac said. "In virtual reality, the app will shrink us down, making us small enough to see the transfer of electric charges." Zac stretched out his arm.

"Alright, you know the drill," he said. "Everybody in!" The kids huddled together.

FLASH!

ZUMMMMMMmmmmmmm...

When the flash cleared, the living room furniture towered over them. It looked huge!

"Whoa, this is crazy!" Marcus shouted. "Are you going to try the balloon trick again, Zac?"

"I sure am!" Zac said. He pulled another balloon from his pocket, blew it up, and knotted it shut.

"Orbit's still taking cover on the other side of the couch," Zac said. They walked over to the dog's flank. It looked like a mountain covered in fur.

Zac rubbed the balloon on Orbit's fur. When he pulled the balloon away, the fur lifted gently along with it! The kids watched as tiny twinkling balls of light began flickering about. "Those are the electrons jumping from the surface of the balloon back to Orbit's fur."

Suddenly, Lucía ran towards Marcus, dragging her socks on the carpet as she went. She reached out to tag him. A small fireball of electrons flew from the tip

of her finger to Marcus's arm.

"OW!" Marcus yelped in surprise. "What's the big idea?" he laughed.

"The big idea is to see the transfer of static electricity, remember?" Lucía teased. Zac dropped the balloon, and soon all the children were dragging their feet on the carpet. They giggled and ran around, tagging each other with tiny fireballs of electricity that jumped from their fingertips.

Chapter 4
Blackout

BANG! A loud crack sounded, and a bright flash filled the room. The house fell suddenly dark. Zac switched off his app, and the kids were back to normal size. All the lights in the house were off. Even the little red light on the television had gone out. Marcus flipped a light switch anxiously, with no effect.

"A lightning strike must have knocked out the power," Zac said. "I think there's a flashlight in the kitchen. The children felt their way down the dark hallway and gathered around the kitchen table. Zac searched the drawers and cabinets for the flashlight.

"Hey, kids," called a voice from the dark hallway.

"Hey, Mom," Zac said. "Do you know where the flashlight is?"

"I'm afraid I don't," said Mrs. Newton. "But we have some glow sticks left over from Halloween." One by one, Mrs. Newton unwrapped the little plastic tubes,

cracked them, and then shook them. The liquid inside began to glow with an eerie green light. She handed the glow sticks out to Zac, Marcus, Ning, and Lucía.

"It's nice to see you all again," Mrs. Newton said. "You're welcome to stay until the storm is over. I'll drive you home when the rain lets up. Call your parents and let them know where you are, so they don't worry. Help yourselves to some snacks!" Mrs. Newton disappeared back down the hallway.

Lucía gazed into her glow stick. "She's right. I need to call my mom. How long do you think it'll take to get the power on?"

Zac held his glow stick in the darkened refrigerator, rummaging around inside by its light. "That depends on what happened. It could have been two things," Zac said. He pulled out a bag of carrot sticks, poured them into a bowl, and set it on the table.

"What two things?" Lucía asked.

"If a lightning bolt hit a tree, the trunk or branches might have fallen on power lines, pulling them down with it." Zac munched on a carrot stick.

"That doesn't sound good," Marcus said.

"Otherwise, a lightning bolt may have struck on or near a power line. The electricity in the lightning bolt is much more powerful than that in the power lines. So a lightning strike can cause a surge, or a sudden increase in electric current. A surge in the power lines can blow the breakers and knock out the power."

"What are breakers?" asked Ning.

"Breakers are like switches on the power lines. When

there's too much electricity, the breakers blow, cutting off the power."

"So they cut the power on purpose?" asked Marcus.

"Kind of," Zac replied. "The blowing of the breakers helps to prevent a surge of current into our houses. Otherwise, it might start fires or electrocute people."

"How do they fix it?" Lucía asked impatiently.

"The utility company will probably send out a worker in a bucket truck," Zac said. "The truck has a 'bucket' attached to a mechanical arm. The worker stands in the bucket. The mechanical arm lifts the bucket, so the worker can reach the power lines."

Lucía peered out the window. "I'd hate to have to work out in that storm."

"If it's a blown breaker," Zac continued, "the worker will either reset or replace it. If it's a downed power line, the worker opens the breakers, cutting off the power to the line that needs repair. Once the power is cut, the worker can safely touch the power line to repair it. Then the worker closes the breakers, and the current flows again."

"We'll just have to wait it out," Lucía said. She pulled her cell phone out to call her mom.

"Oh, no! My battery is dead. I *can't* call my mom," she groaned. "With the power out, I can't charge the battery. How am I going to check in?"

"Maybe we can make a battery and use it to charge your phone," Zac suggested. "My Backspace app still works. Let's go see how the battery was invented. I'll set our destination. Huddle up! Here we go!"

FLASH!

ZUMMMMMMmmmmmmm...

Chapter 5
Animal Electricity

When the flash faded, the kids were standing in the doorway of a science laboratory. Inside, a man in a dusty white wig leaned over the table.

"Oh, no," Zac whispered, checking his phone screen. "We came back too far. The Backspace app dropped us off in Italy, in 1781."

The children peered through the doorway. Outside the laboratory windows, a storm thundered, just like back home. Rain beat against the thin glass, and lightning flashed in the sky. Orbit lay down and covered his ears with his paws.

"What's that guy doing to that dead frog?" Lucía asked with a troubled look.

"That's Luigi Galvani," Zac said. "He's a scientist who studied electrical impulses in living things. His work led to the creation of the battery."

"Let's go talk to him!" said Ning excitedly, bouncing on her toes. "Maybe he'll tell us what the frog is for!"

"Yeah, maybe he can help us figure out how to power my phone," Lucía said.

"Well, if he can't help us with the battery, maybe he can use electricity to fry up some of those frog's legs. I'm starving!" Marcus exclaimed.

"You're always hungry," said Lucía. "And who eats frog legs, anyway? Yuck!"

"A lot of people in Italy eat deep-fried frog legs," Zac explained.

"At my house, we stir fry them with ginger and scallions," added Ning.

"Now I'm really hungry!" Marcus said.

"Let's go," said Zac.

Zac, Lucía, Marcus, and Ning pushed into the laboratory and approached Galvani.

"Uh, hi! Excuse me, Mr. Galvani?" The man jerked up from his work, startled.

"What? Oh, hello. How can I help you?" Galvani looked the kids over with curiosity. "You must be students."

"Yes, exactly!" Zac said quickly. "We're students. We were wondering if we could ask you about the experiment you're working on."

"I suppose I could spare a few moments. What would you like to know, my friends?" Galvani asked. He looked at the kids with a smile.

"What are you doing with that frog?" Ning asked.

"Ah, yes!" Galvani clapped happily. "The frog! I've discovered *animal electricity*."

"Animal electricity?" the children said together.

"You mean there's electricity inside that frog?" Ning asked.

"Sure!" Galvani said. "Inside the nerves and tissues are tiny particles of electricity. When you touch metal to the tissue, it causes electric current to flow. The nerves and muscles come to life with twitches and jerks!"

"How do you do that?" Ning asked.

"You use two different metals—for example, the steel of this knife and the copper of this hook—to conduct the current within the animal."

The children looked on in wonder as Galvani prepared his demonstration. He carefully placed the steel knife and copper hook inside the muscles of the dead frog, which was pinned down on the table in front of him. Suddenly, the legs of the frog began to dance.

"Wow!" the kids exclaimed.

"That's an amazing discovery, Mr. Galvani," Zac said. "We don't want to keep you from your work, though, so we'll be going now. Thank you for showing us your frog."

"Well, if you must go so quickly," Galvani replied. "Nice to see you all! Come by any time! Ciao!"

Zac hurried the others back through the door of Galvani's lab and into the hallway. Galvani waved to

them as they left. Then he turned back to his work with the frog.

"Electricity in living flesh? That reminds me of a horror movie I saw once," Marcus said. "*Frankenstein.*"

"Only Frankenstein's monster was pieced together from parts of dead *people,*" Zac added. "Dr. Frankenstein uses a machine to send electric current from a storm into the body of the monster, bringing it to life."

"Ew!" Lucía said. "That sounds disgusting."

"It is pretty gross," Zac agreed. "But *Frankenstein* is considered one of the first science fiction stories ever. It was written by an English woman named Mary Shelley. She got the idea after she learned about Galvani's work!"

"You know what else?" Zac continued. "Galvani hadn't actually discovered animal electricity, like he thought. He had discovered something else, called *galvanism.*"

"What's galvanism?" Marcus asked.

"Galvanism is the creation of electric current when two different metals are placed in a moist environment," Zac said.

"Like the steel knife and the copper hook in the juicy leg of the frog," Ning chimed in.

"Exactly! Galvani was right about one thing," Zac explained. "It was electricity that caused the frog's muscles to dance and twitch. But he was wrong about where the electricity came from. He thought it came from inside the frog. But it was actually generated by the tools he used to conduct the experiment."

"So Galvani's experiment was a failure," Lucía observed.

"It's true that Galvani didn't discover what he thought he did," said Zac. "But he had discovered something else interesting. Science can be like that. Sometimes, you make a mistake that leads to something new."

"That sounds interesting," Lucía said, "but what about the battery?"

"Good call," Zac replied, typing into the Backspace app. "Let's see if I can adjust the settings to take us to Alessandro Volta. Volta used Galvani's ideas to develop the first battery." Marcus called Orbit out of the corner.

Zac stretched out his arm.

"All right, gather around," he said.

FLASH!

ZUMMMMMMmmmmmmm...

Chapter 6
Battery Power

The friends found themselves in a room fit for a king. It was richly decorated, with life-sized portraits framed in gold. Heavy drapes covered the windows. A group of well-dressed men stood looking at a large tube on a table. Alessandro Volta was standing nearby.

Marcus pointed to another man, in the crowd. "Why does that guy in the funny hat look so familiar?" he asked.

"That's the famous French leader Napoleon!" Lucía responded.

"I knew he looked familiar," Marcus said. "He was one of the greatest military geniuses of all time. What's he doing here?"

"We're in Paris, in 1801," Zac said. "Volta is presenting his invention, the voltaic pile, to Napoleon and a group of men from the National Institute of France. The institute was created in the 1600's to inform the French government about important advances in science."

"Ah, hello, friends!" Alessandro Volta said, holding out his hand to greet Zac, Marcus, Lucía, and Ning. "I'm so happy to see a few young scientists among us! I was just getting ready to present my voltaic pile."

"What's a voltaic pile?" Marcus asked.

"I'll explain from over here." Volta walked behind the table and welcomed everyone to his presentation.

"This magnificent tube is the voltaic pile," Volta explained to the group. "Inside the tube are disks made of the metals zinc and copper. Between each disk is a piece of cardboard soaked in an electrolyte."

Chapter 6

"An electrolyte is a special liquid or gel that contains ions," Zac whispered. "An ion is an electrically charged atom. The ions in the electrolyte help it to conduct electricity."

"These three elements—the two disks and the soaked cardboard between—make up one cell," Volta continued. "By itself, each cell produces only a little electric current. But when you connect many cells together in an organized series, or battery…"

"That's must be where the word *battery* comes from," interrupted Ning.

"Shhhhh…" shushed Lucía.

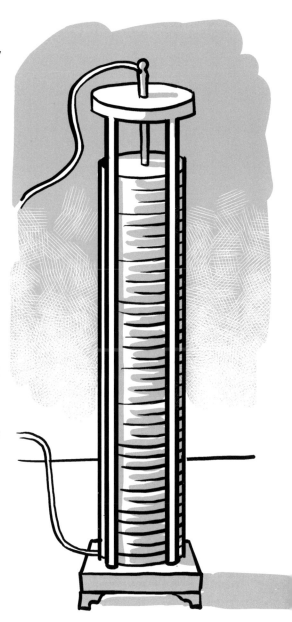

Volta continued, "The more cells there are, the more electric current the battery produces. This invention is the first to provide a steady flow of electricity."

The crowd watched in curiosity as Volta continued. "Wires are attached at the top and the bottom of the tube. You simply connect these wires to whatever you need to power."

"The copper and zinc disks are like the two metals that Galvani used in the frog," Ning said quietly.

"Right," Zac whispered.

"So, Galvani thought there was electricity in the frog, but the electricity came from a chemical reaction between the two metals and the liquid in the frog's body," Lucía said.

"Right," Ning replied. "And in the voltaic pile, the cardboard soaked in electrolytes takes the place of the frog."

"Exactly," said Zac. "That gives me an idea. Let's get back to my house."

Zac tapped the screen of his phone. Volta and Napoleon disappeared, and the children were back in Zac's kitchen.

"Batteries have changed a lot since 1801," Marcus said. "That voltaic pile is way too big to fit in Lucía's phone."

"The voltaic pile can only make so much power, too. If you add too many cells, the pile becomes so heavy that it squeezes out the electrolyte. It stops conducting properly," Zac added. He fumbled through the kitchen drawers.

"But batteries are still based on the same three parts," Zac continued. "Inside a battery's casing, there are two conductors called electrodes. One of the electrodes is positive, and the other is negative."

"How are the positive and negative electrodes different?" Marcus asked.

"Remember those electrons we zapped each other with earlier?" Zac asked.

Marcus nodded. "That was fun!"

"Remember, electrons have a negative charge," Zac continued. "There are electrons in the electrolyte. A chemical reaction at the negative electrode causes electrons to enter the conductor. When you hook up the battery to a device, such as a flashlight or a phone, the electrons flow through it. They flow from the negative electrode, through the device, to the positive electrode. The flow of electrons is an electric current."

Zac opened the darkened refrigerator and looked through the drawers by the light of his glow stick.

"Why do batteries stop working?" Lucía asked.

"It has to do with the chemical reaction that causes electrons to enter the negative electrode," Zac answered. "Eventually, the chemicals have reacted completely. No more chemical reaction. The battery won't work anymore."

Zac grabbed a bowl and dropped a few items into it, then placed it on the kitchen table.

"I'll be right back," Zac said. He disappeared down the hallway, leaving the others peering into the bowl.

"I hope this isn't our snack," Lucía said. In the bowl were a lemon, a nail, and a short length of wire.

"I had to go get my wire strippers from the garage," Zac said, returning to the table. He used the tool to scrape the rubber coating off the end of the copper wire.

"Ning, can you roll this lemon on the table for a minute? We need to break up its insides to get the juices flowing," asked Zac.

"You got it," Ning said, pushing down on the lemon as she rolled it along the table. A fresh, lemony scent soon filled the kitchen. Zac straightened the copper wire and cleaned the nail with a damp paper towel.

"What exactly are we doing?" Marcus asked.

"Making a battery!" Lucía guessed before Zac could reply.

"That's right," said Zac. "The wire is copper, and the nail is coated in zinc. Those two metals, plus the acidic juice from the lemon, equals the perfect combination to produce electricity."

"Let's try it!" Lucía said excitedly.

"Ning, pass the lemon over," said Zac. He plunged the copper wire into the lemon. Close to that, he pushed in the zinc-coated nail.

"Now it's time to test it," Zac said. He reached into his pocket and pulled out a tiny little light, like a Christmas light, with two little wires coming from it. Zac connected one of the wires to the nail and the other to the copper wire. Marcus, Lucía, and Ning gasped as a faint glow came from inside the bulb.

"It works!" Zac said.

"Neat!" cried Ning.

"We made a battery from food!" said Marcus.

Zac picked up his glow stick and resumed fumbling around in the fridge, while Marcus and Lucía took turns testing the battery.

"It's a pretty cool trick," said Marcus, "but that glow isn't very bright."

"Unfortunately, our lemon battery isn't very powerful," Zac admitted.

"Could you make a stronger battery if you added another lemon?" Ning asked.

"Yes, but I can't find any more!" Zac said.

Chapter 7
A Magnetic Idea

"We need more battery power to get this thing working," Lucía said, fumbling with her lifeless phone.

"Don't worry," Ning said, putting her hand on Lucía's shoulder. "The power will be on soon. I'm sure of it."

"We can get electric current from the lemon battery, but it isn't enough to power the phone. And we saw the voltaic pile, but it doesn't have enough power, either. How does the power company make enough electricity to power the whole city?" Marcus asked.

"They have a really big bowl of lemons," Lucía joked. The kids all laughed at the thought.

"Actually, it's magnets," Zac said, as the laughter died down. "They make electricity with magnets."

"Like the magnets on your fridge?" Marcus asked, confused.

"Yeah, like those," Zac said. "But way bigger. I think it's time for another adventure. Let's go!"

FLASH!

ZUMMMMMMmmmmmmm...

The kitchen disappeared, and the kids were in another strange laboratory. A thin, middle-aged man stood working over a tabletop littered with odd-looking devices. The children recognized a voltaic pile, but there was also something that looked like a small life preserver and a machine with a large disk. The table was scattered with spools of wire, a magnetic compass, hand tools, notebooks, and other items useful to an inventor.

The room glowed yellow-orange with candlelight. There was no storm outside this laboratory, but a gentle breeze blew in. It caused the light to flicker as the scientist worked.

"That's Michael Faraday," Zac said. "He's the scientist that discovered a special connection between magnetism and electricity."

"Just curious," Ning said, "where are we, exactly?"

"London, 1831," Zac said. "We're at the headquarters of the Royal Institution of Great Britain, one of the world's great scientific organizations."

"That's right," Faraday said from his workbench. "I worked my way up here, starting as a laboratory assistant. Now I'm the superintendent, and I can use the labs and equipment for my own experiments."

Faraday glanced up from his work and gave the kids a smile. "What brings you all here?" he asked.

"Hello, Mr. Faraday," Zac said. "We were wondering if you might have a moment to explain how magnets can be used to make electricity."

"Oh, of course, my friends," Faraday replied. "I've discovered that moving a magnet inside a coil of wire creates electric current in the wire."

"What's that on the table?" Ning asked.

"It's a tube made of paper," Faraday said. "I've wrapped wire around the tube and hooked each end

of the wire to a galvanometer. That's a tool that detects electric current. The needle on the galvanometer moves when it picks up a current."

Faraday made a few notes in his notebook. Then the scientist picked up his tube and coil and began moving a magnet through its center. Faraday smiled as the needle of the galvanometer twitched to life. The magnet was producing an electric current in the coil!

Michael Faraday laughed out loud with delight. Zac and his friends cheered Faraday's discovery.

"The faster you move the magnet, the stronger the current," said Faraday. "Moving it by hand, I cannot create much current. But I'm working on a device to turn the magnet faster, increasing the current produced."

"Thank you for showing us how it works," Lucía said.

"Ah, my pleasure!" Michael Faraday replied.

"We'll leave you to your work now," Zac said.

Everyone waved goodbye as they left the science lab.

"That's the idea behind the electric generator, right?" Marcus asked. "It's how modern generators work?"

"Yes," Zac said. "The power plants that make electricity for our houses and businesses use generators that are much bigger versions of Faraday's idea. Let's go back to the kitchen. Then I'll take you on a tour of the power plant near my house."

Zac tapped the button on his app, and the laboratory disappeared. The kids were back at the kitchen table.

"Let me pull up the power plant on my app, and we'll walk through it virtually. It's safer than wandering around a power plant in real life," Zac said.

Moments later, Zac used his phone to project an image of the power plant on the wall.

"This is the power plant a few miles from here," Zac said. There were metal tubes everywhere, and large towers with steam billowing from their tops.

"Whoa," Ning said. "This is impressive. I never knew what it looked like in there. It's a maze of metal!"

"Yeah," Lucía agreed. "It feels like we're actually there!"

Zac tapped the screen of his phone, and the projected view entered a brick building. Inside was a huge room full of giant machinery. More metal pipes crisscrossed the room.

"See those pipes," Zac said. "They're full of hot steam. Most power plants use heat to make electricity. They burn coal, natural gas, or oil to create the steam that powers the generators."

"Power plants can be powered by flowing water, too," Marcus added. "I visited the Hoover Dam with my family a few years ago. Plants that are powered by water are called hydroelectric power plants."

"That's right," Zac said. "There are wind-powered plants, too." The virtual tour continued through the hall of the power plant. It paused beside a giant metal tube that was bigger than car.

"Inside this metal cover, or casing, is the turbine," Zac explained. "The turbine is like a giant fan, with hundreds of little blades. The steam is pumped through pipes into the turbine casing. The steam pushes on the blades of the turbine, causing it to spin. The spinning turns a giant shaft that's connected to the generator…"

Zac paused as the view shifted from the turbine to another large casing next to it.

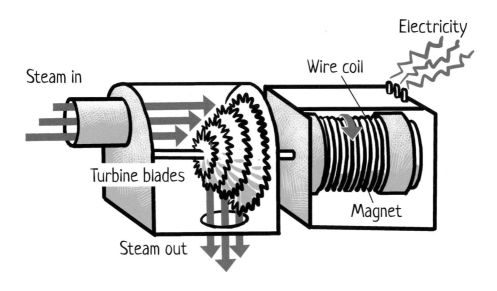

"Here's the generator," Zac said.

"Wow," Ning exclaimed. "I wonder what it looks like inside there."

Zac pressed a few buttons, and the virtual image moved inside the generator casing.

"Look at all the wire around that magnet," Lucía said. "That magnet must be the size of a hippo."

The kids looked closely at the layers of wire coiled around the giant magnet.

"See, the magnet spins inside the coil and generates electric current," Zac said. "Wires conduct that current from the generator to the power lines."

"These wires don't go straight to our houses, though," Zac continued. "The voltage—or strength—of the electricity is much too high. If current from this cable went into our houses, it would fry all our appliances, just like a lightning strike. First, the high-voltage electricity goes through transformers."

"Now that I know about," said Marcus. "Those are like robots that turn into cars, right?" he joked.

"Very funny," Zac replied. "These transformers are devices that reduce the current to a lower voltage. Then, it's sent through power lines to our houses."

The kids took one last look at the generator before Zac closed the app, ending their virtual tour.

Chapter 8
Cracking the Code

Marcus picked up the lemon battery from the table and examined it thoughtfully. "It's hard to believe that electricity and magnetism are so closely related."

"It's true," said Zac. "Let me show you something." Zac took the lemon from Marcus and pulled out the nail and copper wire. He carefully wrapped the copper wire around the nail. "Now, if I only had a battery…" he mused.

"Why?" said Ning.

Zac explained. "If I could connect both ends of this wire to a battery, the current flowing through the wire would turn the nail into a magnet."

"Really?" asked Lucía.

"Yes," said Zac. "It's a kind of magnet called an electromagnet. And long before there were telephones, people used them to communicate."

The children huddled together, already guessing Zac's next move. He pulled out his phone and opened the Backspace app.

FLASH!

ZUMMMMMMmmmmmmm...

The kitchen vanished, and the friends found themselves in a workshop. Painted canvases leaned against one wall. On the opposite side of the room was a gray-haired man in a vest and shirtsleeves. He worked at a table cluttered with wires and tools. Next to him stood a wooden frame. A long piece of wood dangled down its center.

"That's Samuel Morse," Zac said quietly, "the inventor of the telegraph. It's a device that uses electric current to send messages along wires. It's the 1830's, and that's the first model of a telegraph he built." Zac pointed to the wooden frame. "He didn't have a lot of money to spend on scientific equipment. Instead, he used things he already had here in his art studio to build a model. The model proved that his idea could work."

"Were there other versions of the telegraph?" Ning asked.

"Yes!" Samuel Morse replied. "No need to whisper here, friends! Other people are working on the same idea—sending messages by wire using electric current. But I will be the first to make the device practical by combining it with a special code."

"Can you tell us about the model?" Marcus asked.

"Of course," Morse said. "The frame is made from a canvas stretcher, a device I use to prepare canvases for my paintings. From the frame's top, I've hung a wooden arm. Below is a wheel. I stretch a piece of paper over the wheel to record the code."

"How does that work?" Ning asked.

"This electromagnet controls the movement of the wooden arm. When I provide current to the electromagnet, then cut the current, it moves the arm across the paper-covered wheel at the bottom. The movement of the arm makes a mark on the paper," Morse said.

The friends watched as Samuel Morse used the wires on his homemade electromagnet to stop and start the flow of electric current.

"This is just a rough model," Morse said. "I plan on putting together a better device once I've demonstrated the basics."

The children watched as Morse continued to explain.

"If I just quickly tap the current on and off, the wooden arm moves just slightly, making a little mark on the paper." Morse said. He tapped on his electromagnet. The machine made a series of short marks on the paper.

"If I hold the current on for a longer time, the arm swings farther, leaving a bigger mark," Morse explained.

Morse tapped the magnet a few more times and retrieved the paper from beneath the wooden arm. He held it up to a lantern, and the children could see that the marks formed a code made up of dots and dashes.

"See here? A perfect, coded message sent along the wire," Morse said.

He smiled, tucked a new piece of paper into the telegraph, and began working with the electromagnet again.

"Thank you, Mr. Morse," Zac said. "It's an amazing

model. I can't wait to see the final product."

"Ah, yes," Morse said, "It shall be revolutionary!"

"It certainly will," Marcus said. "Until e-mail and cell phones come along!"

Morse looked at Marcus, confused.

"Have a good day, sir," Zac said.

With a push of a button, Samuel Morse disappeared. The kids were back at the kitchen table.

Suddenly, Ning's eyes lit up. She pulled a folded piece of yellowed paper from her pocket. It was the paper she and Zac had been examining earlier.

"That's it, Zac!" she cried excitedly. "This paper I found in my attic, the one we were looking at when Orbit took off. It has marks just like the ones on Morse's little paper strip!"

The friends gathered around, peering at the coded message with curiosity.

"Great thinking, Ning!" Zac replied. "We definitely have to decode that."

"Wait," Lucía said. "Is that really how people sent messages? They stood there tapping wires on an electromagnet?"

"Not exactly," Zac said. "Morse and Alfred Vail—a partner who came along later—developed a device called a key. It's a little wooden base with a small metal arm. When you tap the metal arm, it sends electric current into a wire connected to the key."

"Kind of like a light switch?" asked Lucía.

"That's a good comparison," said Zac. "And the wires were just like our telephone wires, strung by poles across the land. Some of the wires were underground, too. The current from the key runs along the wire, from one telegraph station to the next."

"How do they decode the message?" Lucía asked.

"At the receiving end, there is a device called a sounder. The sounder had an iron bar and an electromagnet," Zac said. "When the current came into the sounder, it made the iron bar bump into the electromagnet, creating a clicking sound. The length of the click determined if the signal was a dot or a dash."

"Thank goodness for phones and e-mail. It's so much easier than having to rely on a code sent across wires," Marcus said.

"Yeah, thank goodness for technology," Ning agreed, "but can we decode this message?"

"We can!" Zac said, "The code that Morse was using became known as Morse code. I think I have a book about it in my room."

"Perfect!" Ning said.

Zac left for a moment, returning to the table with the book. Marcus held a glow stick over Zac's shoulder, lighting the book. Zac flipped through the pages in search of the code key.

"Aha!" Zac said finally. "Here it is." He passed

a pencil and a piece of paper to Ning. They hunched over the old message and the code key, working together to match each pattern of dots and dashes with a letter of the alphabet.

"This is so cool," Ning said softly as she stared at the message. "I think we've got it."

"What does it say?" Lucía asked.

"You read it, Ning," Zac said.

"Okay. It says *Dear Connie, We have arrived in San Pablo Bay. We hear there is a fishing village here where we can earn extra money. Will be on our way back to you soon. Love, Jun.*"

"Who are they?" Marcus asked.

"Jun and Connie are my great-great-great grandparents," Ning said. "My family moved to San Francisco from China around the time of the Gold Rush, in 1849. My grandmother must have stayed in the city, while my grandfather traveled to find work."

"Wow, they were part of a lot of history," Marcus said.

"I can't believe we had this message in my attic. I can't wait to get home and show this to my mother." Ning tucked the papers into her pocket and walked over to the window to look outside. "I wish this rain would let up."

Chapter 9
Current Events

Zac washed his hands in the kitchen sink. He used the last paper towel to dry off. As he went to throw away the empty roll, an idea struck. He began wrapping the cardboard tube with copper wire he found in the drawer.

"Lucía," he asked, "will you grab me a fork from the silverware drawer?"

"Sure thing," Lucía replied. She opened the drawer and began rummaging around.

"Ah, found one. What else?" Lucía asked.

"There are some bar magnets and rubber bands in the next drawer up," Zac said. He continued winding the wire around the tube.

"Grab two magnets and rubber band them together for me, please."

"I have junk like this in my kitchen too," Lucía said

sarcastically. "It's a regular inventor's workshop." She grinned as she gathered the supplies. She put the magnets together as Zac requested.

"That should be good," Zac said, admiring the copper wire he had just finished wrapping. Carefully, he pulled the coil of wire off the tube.

"We'll slide the handle of the fork between these magnets, then put the whole thing inside the copper coil. The coiled wire should hold it all in place while we turn the fork."

Zac began spinning the fork with his fingertips.

"Lucía, hand me your phone charger," Zac said. Lucía passed the charger to Zac. Zac connected each end of the wire coil to one prong of the charger's plug. He began spinning the fork again with his fingertips. He looked at the phone's screen hopefully. It remained blank.

"It's not working," Lucía said. "Maybe we need more power. Did I see a treadmill in your living room?"

"Yes," Zac said with a curious look. "We might be able to use that. Let's go." Everyone grabbed their glow sticks and followed Zac into the corner of the living room, where the treadmill stood hidden in the dark.

"There's no electricity, though. How will that help us if we can't turn it on?" Ning asked.

"I can open the side cover and switch the machine to manual mode, so that the belt turns freely. That way, we can move the belt ourselves, without the motor."

Zac pulled open the plastic cover on the side of the treadmill. Marcus and Lucía shined their glow sticks so he could see what he was doing.

"There. I think I've got it," he said. "Who wants to get on?"

"I will!" Ning replied, hopping onto the treadmill. "You know I love to run!"

"Okay, everybody, stand back!" said Zac. "Now start by walking."

"It's stiff, but it's moving." Ning said. She started running. The treadmill's belt thumped noisily. Zac used his glow stick to find a roller near the edge of the treadmill.

"Pass me the generator, please," Zac said.

Marcus passed the little hand-made generator and the attached phone to Zac.

"The rollers that the belt moves on are made of rubber," Zac explained. "I can stick the fork into the roller. It will spin without us holding onto it. Stop running for a second, Ning."

Ning stopped. Zac found a spot in the center of the wheel and jammed the fork into the rubber.

"That feels pretty secure. Ning, start walking."

Ning began walking. The roller began to turn, and the fork turned with it. The magnet spun inside the coil of wire. In a few moments, the phone's low-battery light flickered on.

"Yes! It's working! Hand me those books from the

coffee table, Marcus," Zac said.

Marcus passed a stack of books to Zac. Zac propped the generator and the phone on top of the books and carefully pulled his hands away. The coil rested on the books, while the magnets continued to spin.

"It's still going to take a while to generate enough power to turn the phone on," Zac said.

The kids sat quietly as Ning walked on the treadmill next to them. Even over her thumping footfalls, they could hear the rumbling thunder and rain hitting the rooftop.

"It was a dark and stormy night…." Marcus said in a spooky voice. He cackled like a witch, and everyone laughed.

"Actually, if you want to hear something creepy, I can tell you about killer electricity," Zac said.

"What's that?" Ning asked from the treadmill.

"Okay, I'm going to tell you a story," Zac replied.

Everyone scooted closer as Ning continued walking.

"Thomas Edison was a famous American inventor. We know him as the inventor of the light bulb, among other things. He also developed the first power plants."

"Like the power plant we visited?" Ning asked.

"Yes, the only difference is the type of electric current that's used," Zac said. "Edison worked with direct current—often abbreviated *DC*."

"What's direct current?" Marcus asked.

"Direct current is electric current that flows only one way. It leaves the power source and moves in one direction along the wire," Zac replied.

"Just like the current from our battery," Lucía observed.

"That's right," said Zac. "The problem with direct current is that it easily loses power as it travels long distances. So, your house would have to be pretty close to a power plant to get enough electric power. Direct current can also create a lot of heat. Too much heat can break light bulbs and other devices."

"Is there something else to use?" Lucía asked.

"There's another kind of current called *alternating current,* or AC. It was developed by Nikola Tesla, a Serbian scientist who came to the United States."

"How is alternating current different?" Ning asked.

"Instead of flowing in one direction, alternating current reverses its flow many times a second. The current travels back and forth along the wires. Alternating current is easier to generate, and it is easier to get it up to higher voltages. High-voltage AC can travel great distances with little loss of energy."

"So, whose idea was the best?" Marcus asked.

"Alternating current won out, and that's what our power plants use today. But it wasn't an easy victory," Zac said. "Edison started a campaign to convince people that alternating current was dangerous. He even electrocuted stray animals in public using AC."

"What? That's terrible!" Lucía exclaimed.

"Edison wanted people to convince people that alternating current was dangerous, so they would choose direct current. His employees even used AC to develop the electric chair, a device for executing condemned criminals," Zac said.

"But another inventor, George Westinghouse, liked Tesla's idea. Together, they won a contract to provide electric power for the World's Columbian Exposition. The exposition was like a giant fair, held in Chicago in 1893. It was meant to show off amazing things. One of the major attractions was electric lighting, which was still new. Hey, let's see if Orbit will run the treadmill for a while. I want to show you all something."

"Orbit, come here boy!" Marcus shouted. Orbit trotted into the living room happily. Ning hopped off the treadmill. Lucía urged the dog onto the belt.

"Okay, walk!" Zac commanded. Orbit stood and looked at him, letting out a confused bark.

"What if we hang a dog treat in front of him?" Marcus asked. Zac's face lit up.

"Great idea, Marcus!" Zac ran to the kitchen for a dog biscuit. He tied it to a string, which he hung from the front of the treadmill. Orbit licked his chops.

"Hold on, boy," Zac said. "Now, walk." Orbit lunged forward and grabbed the treat. The belt didn't move.

"Hmmm. That was a total fail," said Zac, disappointed.

"What if we get the belt started for him?" Ning said. She stepped on the treadmill behind Orbit and began walking. The belt began to move, and the dog trotted

along. Ning hopped off, and Orbit continued walking.

Zac tied another dog treat to the treadmill. Orbit quickened his pace.

"Quick! Everyone line up! We're going to the 1893 World's Columbian Exposition!" Zac said.

The friends lined up in the darkened room. Zac pressed the button.

FLASH!

ZUMMMMMmmmmmmm...

The living room became a broad plaza at sunset. Thousands of unlit lights hung above them. A huge Ferris wheel stood nearby—larger than any they had ever seen. It stood ready to carry passengers into the twilit sky. Huge white buildings towered around the children. Men in fitted suits and ladies in billowing dresses flocked to stands selling food and other treats.

"Who's that?" Marcus asked, pointing to a man standing on stage with wires in his hand.

"That's Nikola Tesla," Zac said. "And that's Grover Cleveland, president of the United States of America."

The president reached down and turned a golden key. Suddenly, 100,000 lamps lit up the fair. The crowd gasped in awe at the flood of light.

"The show's not over yet," Zac whispered.

Tesla held tight to the wire. An assistant flipped a switch, and high-voltage electric current surged through his body. After a few seconds, he dropped the wire, apparently unharmed. The crowd cheered wildly.

"Wow! Tesla survived!" Ning cheered.

"He risked his own life to reassure people that alternating current was safe. It was a dangerous risk, but he got lucky," Zac said. "Don't try that at home."

"Uh, before we go, can we sample some of the food from those stands?" Marcus asked.

Zac laughed. "Sure. Virtual junk food won't give you a tummy ache. But, be quick. I bet Orbit's getting tired."

Marcus quickly passed a few tables, grabbing a bite from each. With a grin, he ran back to meet his friends. Lucía rolled her eyes at Marcus and laughed.

Zac pressed the button, and the fair was gone. They were back in the living room. Orbit was panting, still trotting on the treadmill.

Chapter 10
Power Up

Orbit continued to jog along on the treadmill. "Good dog, Orbit!" Zac said. He gave the dog's back a friendly scratch.

"What's that smell?" Marcus said, excited. "It smells like chocolate!"

"Marcus, when you're hungry, everything smells like chocolate to you," Lucía teased.

"Let's go see," Zac said. Ning, Lucía, and Marcus followed Zac into the kitchen. They found a warm pot of hot chocolate on the stove.

"Your mom must have made that," Ning said. "But how? The power is out."

"We have a gas stove," Zac explained.

"Your mom's the best," Marcus said.

Zac carefully poured the hot chocolate into four mugs. Suddenly, the kids heard a series of faint beeps from the living room.

"No way! Is that my phone?" Lucía asked. She ran to the living room and unplugged it from the homemade generator.

"Great job, Orbit!" she said, patting the dog on his head. "Here you go, boy." She untied the treat from the string and tossed it to him. "You've earned it," she said. Orbit chewed noisily. Then he followed Lucía back into the kitchen. He curled up on his bed in the corner.

"I can't believe it worked!" Lucía exclaimed. "I have a text from my mom."

"She wants to know why Marcus and I aren't at his house. I'll text her back and let her know we're here.

Thanks for helping me get my phone working again, Zac!"

"No problem," Zac said. "All in a day's work."

Lucía put her phone down with a sigh of relief. She lifted her cup and took a sip of the warm, rich hot chocolate.

"Yum. This is amazing," Lucía said.

"But don't you wish you could have had some of those frog legs from Galvani's lab?" Ning asked with a giggle.

"Yeah, that would've been delicious!" Marcus chimed in. "That was my favorite part of today. It was interesting to see how he came up with the idea of animal electricity."

"My favorite part was watching Ben Franklin fly his kite," Lucía said. "I'm going to do a science report about *him*."

"Yeah! Ben was really cool," Ning agreed. "I liked Samuel Morse the most, of course, because he helped me decode that message from my great-great-great grandfather."

"I liked visiting the Columbian Exposition. Tesla really did light up the world with alternating current. After all, that's what most power companies use today," Zac said.

Suddenly the lights flickered on. The kids squinted, laughing in surprise at their suddenly bright surroundings.

"Sounds like you kids have had quite the adventure

today," Zac's mom said. She walked into the kitchen with a friendly smile.

"Thank you for the hot chocolate, Mrs. Newton," Ning said.

"Yeah, thank you!" said Marcus. "It's delicious!"

"It looks like the storm is letting up. I can take you all home in about 10 minutes. I just have a few things to finish up in my office," Mrs. Newton said.

"That'll be great, Mom," Zac said. "Just enough time to finish this hot chocolate!"

"Looks like Orbit enjoyed his adventure today, too," Marcus said with a laugh. The dog was lying sprawled out on his side in the corner of the kitchen snoring. His feet still twitched in a running motion.

"He must be dreaming that he's chasing a rabbit," Zac said.

"Or electrons," Marcus joked.

The friends sat around the table sipping their hot chocolate. The thunder and lightning had stopped. There was a gentle patter on the roof as the last of the rain passed overhead. Zac tapped away on his cell phone, taking notes from the day's adventure. Suddenly, Ning looked puzzled.

"What is it?" asked Zac.

"Well," Ning replied, "that generator you made was pretty clever, Zac, but there's one thing I can't figure out. If you're such a genius, why didn't you just let Lucía use your cell phone to text her mom?"

A stunned look crossed Zac's face. He blushed bright red from ear to ear. "Um, um," he stammered. Finally he blurted out, "Who wants more hot chocolate? I'll pour." The four friends broke into laughter.

Meet the Scientists

Benjamin Franklin

Benjamin Franklin (1706–1790) was a master of many things, including politics and science. He was a founding father of the United States. As a scientist, he was a leader in the study of electricity.

Luigi Galvani

Luigi Galvani (1737–1798) was an Italian physician who discovered galvanism, the production of an electric current when two different metals contact a moist environment.

Alessandro Volta

Alessandro Volta (1745–1827), an Italian inventor, developed one of the first effective electrical batteries, the voltaic pile. The volt, a unit of measurement for electrical charge, was named after him.

Nikola Tesla

Nikola Tesla (1856–1943), an inventor from Serbia, became a pioneer in electrical technology. He is known for creating systems to produce and use alternating current (AC), the form widely used around the world today.

Michael Faraday

Michael Faraday (1791–1867), an English physicist, discovered *electromagnetism,* the combined effect of electricity and magnetism. He found that moving a coil of wire around a magnet produced an electric current.

Samuel Morse

Samuel Morse (1791–1872) was an American inventor who patented the first successful electric telegraph in 1840. His development of the telegraph and Morse code allowed people to communicate more quickly and easily.

Glossary

alternating current an electric current that reverses flow many times per second

breaker a device that cuts off the flow of electric current, helping to prevent a power surge

conductor a material that can carry an electric current

current a flow of electricity

direct current a steady electric current that flows in one direction

electrocution injury or death by electric shock

electrode a conductor through which current enters or leaves an electric device

electrolyte a liquid or paste that conducts electric current

electromagnet a magnet that is activated by the presence of an electric current

electron a tiny particle carrying a negative electric charge

insulator a material that prevents the passage of electric current

ion an electrically charged atom or group of atoms

particle any one of the extremely small units of which all matter is composed

proton a tiny particle carrying a positive electric charge

selfie an informal self-portrait, usually taken with a cell phone

static electricity the accumulation of an electric charge within a material

surge a sudden increase in electric current

virtual created and existing only in a computer—like the historical scenes visited in Zac's Backspace app

volt a measure of the strength of an electric charge

voltaic pile a battery made up of a pile of plates of two different metals, such as copper and zinc, separated by disks soaked in an electrolyte

Additional Resources

Books

DK Eyewitness Books: Electricity
Steve Parker (DK Children, 2013)

Electrical Wizard: How Nikola Tesla Lit Up the World
Elizabeth Rusch (Candlewick, 2015)

Magic School Bus and the Electric Field Trip
Joanna Cole and Bruce Degan (Scholastic, 1999)

Your Guide to Electricity and Magnetism (Drawn to Science: Illustrated Guides to Key Science Concepts)
Gill Arbuthnott (Crabtree Publishing, 2017)

Websites

The Exploratorium
https://www.exploratorium.edu/explore/electricity-magnetism

The Exploratorium is full of science to explore with a whole section dedicated to electricity and magnetism, plus many more videos, experiments, and activities to try at home.

Khan Academy
https://www.khanacademy.org/

Explore Khan Academy's numerous videos, worksheets, and articles about electricity and many other science-related topics.

Royal Institution of Great Britain
http://www.rigb.org/

Explore Michael Faraday's Magnetic Laboratory and learn about the discoveries made by him and other scientists who lived and worked at the Institution.

Index

alternating current 80, 81, 85, 89, 93
atoms 23, 24, 26, 27, 47
batteries 46–53, 63
breakers 34–36
clouds 10, 26
conductors 16, 49, 50
direct current 79, 81
Edison, Thomas 79–81
electrodes 49, 50
electrolytes 46–50
electromagnets 63, 66, 67, 69, 70
electrons 25, 26, 27, 30, 50
Faraday, Michael 55–58, 93
Franklin, Benjamin 12, 15–21, 92
Galvani, Luigi 37–44, 48, 92
generators 58, 60, 61, 73–78
insulators 20
lightning 9–11, 15, 17, 18, 20, 21, 26, 34
magnets 54–58, 61, 63, 66, 67, 69, 70
Morse, Samuel 64–69
morse code 67–71
power lines 34–36, 61
power plants 58–62, 79, 80
static electricity 23, 27–31
Tesla, Nikola 80, 81, 83–85, 93
Volta, Alessandro 44–48, 92
voltaic pile 46–49